ARTIFICIAL

INTELLIGENCE

BY

TONY SAYERS

ABOUT THE AUTHOR

Tony Sayers is a passionate activist, vlogger, writer, and public speaker who in 2013 started to become aware of the deeper goings-on within this World and the hidden hands that control it. Since having these realisations he has been relentless in his work to expose the levels of corruption in society in an attempt to help others open their eyes. He is driven by doing what he can in his own way to help future generations enjoy a better

World. His work has been mainly focused on human psychology, mind control, and spiritual laws. He is now progressing into technological, metaphysical manipulations, and energy healing work.

Born in Southend on Sea, Essex, UK he enjoyed a good childhood, although he found school quite challenging with other students and somewhat boring. His questioning of what is 'normal' had subconsciously already begun. From school, Tony went traveling when he was 21 which was a huge learning curve where he felt he got a real education observing how other cultures lived, and the vast differences between the developed and non-developed World. He also traveled to Nepal and researched Buddhism, which at the time which was to sew a spiritual seed in him that was to germinate later in life. After this period he went on to work in many standard jobs in both the Banking and Estate Agency Worlds, but never truly felt fulfilled, and feeling as if he was just going through the motions of life. It was in this period where he was so downbeat in the rigorous daily grind he started to ask the big questions in life which ultimately led him to these greater understandings about himself and the World, the learning is still going on today.

Sometimes controversial Tony is raw in how he expresses himself and his truth but is always coming from a place of care and desire for positive change. Tony has appeared on radio shows and spoke publicly which can be found on YouTube. He has his own website which is http://www.transcendingtimes.org where all his work can be found. To Subscribe To subscribe to his free weekly newsletter which has blogs, vlogs, media announcements and information on up and coming books just join here https://transcendingtimes.org/subscribe-to-newsletters/

Tony has authored other books

including 'Are You Living Or Just Existing?'and 'Ten Life Hacks To Beat The Matrix' both of which are available on Amazon. You can subscribe to his weekly mailing list here https://transcendingtimes.org/subscribe-to-newsletters/

INTRODUCTION

It really is extraordinary to think just how much this World has changed even in the last 15-20 years or so, can you even imagine a time when we all didn't have a mobile phone in our hand? Hours, days, months, and even years are spent by many people staring at screens on handheld devices, laptops, and computers, there is a high chance that you may even be reading this book on some kind of electronic device. (i'm not complaining!)

There seems to be a march towards automation on so many levels of society as we are seeing artificial intelligence start to dominate over humans in many different ways. But is it even necessarily a good thing? This obsession with technology has already driven us into almost destroying the Planet with modern ways in which to rape the Earth of her natural resources which saw the dawning of the industrial revolution.

Modern warfare could easily drive us to distinction if this technology gets into the wrong hands (some could argue the fact that it already is in the wrong hands!) It's not about duels with swords on a battlefield anymore, one look at the website of the artificial intelligence arm of the US military DARPA and it sends shivers down the spine.

This is why soldiers being called 'heroes' is so laughable these days, they're invading Countries they have no right to be in with the highest possible technology around and bombing goat farmers who have nothing more than stick and stones half the time! This is all on the say so of some corrupt politician who has been given a backhander by the weapons manufacturers and oil companies.

So one of our biggest concerns really

should be not only about the technology and AI itself, but really we need to be questioning the hands in which it is being used, and I for one do not trust them one iota!

This book really seeks to ask the questions about this invasion of technology. Because it is packaged up for us in a way in which we have fallen in love with it. But like any relationship shouldn't we get to know it a bit first? It seems to have been love at first sight but what are the consequences as we become more 'plugged in' than ever and disconnected Nature? Of course, it's not all bad but we need to probe deeper now the honeymoon period is over

CONTENTS

Not So Social Media

Artificial Intelligence is, without a shadow of a doubt, becoming more and more prominent in our lives, we are surrounded by technology the scale of which some of it is quite remarkable. We live in a World now dominated by gadgets and gizmos that basically have the capacity to communicate with each other and with the user.

It has become so advanced at such an alarming rate you have to wonder where it will end, and more importantly what are the effects going to be for humanity as a whole? Have we become so addicted and bedazzled by this new technology that we have been blinded by it? It seems to have the World's population in a trance.

Just walk down any street and you

will see droves of people just staring down at their phones, sit in any restaurant and you will see couples doing the same. For sure we are 'connected' in one aspect, for example, whilst living in Thailand I have the ability to connect with someone in Colombia yet I might be completely disconnected from the person sitting in front of me!

It sounds like a joke but really it's not, there appears to be an artificial connectedness as well as an artificial intelligence. Its real but at the same time, it's not because you're missing the physical human interaction that we all crave.

Our lives have become such that we obsess about what hundreds and thousands of 'followers' think about us, desperately trying to get more 'likes,' 'retweets' or whatever the dopamine hit maybe at the time depending on which platform you're using.

Ultimately that is the science behind it, every time you receive a 'like' from somebody you get an injection of dopamine to your brain, which is the feel-good chemical. It's like a little reassurance that someone out there in the vacuum of Facebook or Instagram 'approves' of whatever it is you have said or indeed made for dinner!

Again this is very clever because it plays on most human beings psyches of feeling inadequate or not good enough due to unhealed childhood issues. So what happens then? If you're constantly receiving those 'pats on the back' so to speak then it becomes an addiction, it becomes very difficult to wean off from.

Especially if most people are not giving themselves that reassurance and love themselves, or someone in their life is not either.

I'm not professing to be perfect here, I use social media extensively for my activism and blogging, I have been caught in these traps from time to time, and I probably still spend too much time on social media, but at the same time I can see it for what it is and what it is doing to people, and how it is being used for much more sinister reasons that I will go into further in this book.

The fact is that people are living their lives on social media and not living their real lives. So much of it is fake too, everyone has the perfect marriage, the perfect children, and that leads other people to feel insecure and doubtful about their own lives.

It is also so easy to star smear campaigns about a person too, people hanging their dirty washing on the line, it can be like the online version of the Jerry Springer show!

What it has also triggered in the human psyche is a narcissism which is now totally out of control, underpinned by the rise of the 'selfie' or people down the gym posting constantly of what they look like. For many it is all about how you look, selfies but no knowledge of 'self'.

Maybe it appears that I am just moaning, people are enjoying themselves right so what's the problem? The question is multifaceted in and of itself, firstly to have that level of obsession with one's looks is shallow to the extreme, it also plays into the dynamic that our outer shell i.e our human body is more important than our internal World, the emotions we need to deal with to be truly happy, the knowledge we need to gain in order to understand ourselves and the World around us. If only the Worlds psychotherapists offices were filled up like the gyms were! We certainly wouldn't be having so many damaging and toxic relationships that's for sure.

Selfie to me means 'selfish', I don't mean the people that post the odd selfie because I do that myself from time to time, I'm talking about the constant bombardment day after day of pouting and posing. What else are these people actually offering the World other than a nice pair of boobs, or big muscles? Who really gives a fuck?

Some of these people have millions of followers with hungry men drooling over nothing. I sometimes think what I could do with all of these followers! A person could make a huge impact on peoples lives. I'm not saying they are all like that, unfortunately, we live in a World that we have to generalise with huge trends like this. My point is that this narcissism is like cancer in society and its growing out of hand. This is because of these platforms and devices that have appeared on the scene. I seriously do not remember such an obsession with looks back in the 80s!

This 'selfie generation' epitomises for me a generation that really didn't give a fuck when the World was descending into chaos,

I outline most of this in my previous book 'Are you living or just existing?' There is so much going on around us right now with constant Wars, financial crashes, and austerity this generation doesn't seem to care less, maybe thats part of the programming infused within social media itself?

Get people so self-centered and focused on me, me, me that the 1% can do pretty much whatever they want unchecked. Its symbolic of this 'Kim Kardashian society' that has elevated mindlessness and stupidity as king alongside fake beauty.

I have to laugh when I think about the notorious 'selfie sticks' where JUST IN CASE you find yourself in the completely desperate situation of not being able to take a proper selfie you now can with this fake extended arm! Genius. Thank God that this was invented, what would our ego's do missing that little stroke we would have got from potentially missing that picture!

I have to laugh when I think about the notorious selfie sticks where JUST IN CASE you find yourself in the completely desperate situation of not being able to take a proper selfie you now can with this fake arm! Genius. Thank God that this was invented, what would our ego's do missing that little stroke we would have got from that potentially missing picture!

A funny story I was once in Iceland visiting the stunning 'Blue Lagoon' which is a geothermal spa, extremely relaxing to bathe in and just chill out. The last place you would want to be taking pictures in because of A its water and B why would you?

Well, there I was floating on my back when this couple waded in holding their selfie sticks up in the air trying not to get their devices wet poting away, good job they didn't drop their phones in the water because about 150 people could have been electrocuted!

My point really is here that technology used in this way has not really been positive for our spiritual growth. It is bringing out the absolute worst traits out in people as far as I can see. This is not going to change anytime soon with kids being able to download apps before they can name the wildlife in their own back gardens and that's sad to see. Parents seem to be encouraging this and nobody seems to bat an eyelid or even care. As long as you have that perfect picture that's all that seems to matter.

CENSORSHIPAND

SUPPRESSION

Now it is my opinion that there are a number of reasons for this new wave of social conditioning. To turn our attention on shallow matters like looks taking preference over more important aspects of our humanity, but also for a much more sinister reason too and that being facial recognition. Anyone with half a finger on the pulse will know that we are now living in a surveillance state with increasing censorship of anyone that doesn't spout the mainstream rhetoric.

Anyone posting anything even slightly controversial can expect Facebook bans, and there are algorithms in place now which ensure only a very select few people see any of your posts. As I write, there is a daily increase of entire YouTube channels with thousands of followers being shut down. People who speak out against the system are forced into an echo chamber where they repeat to people who already know what is going on, however, If you post a picture of your dog or breakfast you will be seen and heard, question the State or anything related and you will be almost talking to yourself.

They sell it to us that they want us to 'see more of what we want' when in reality it is that they want us to see less of what we NEED to see!

I have recently had 5000 Facebook followers literally deleted over a period of 4 months, my YouTube followers are culled every time they start to rise. I have had about six 30 day Facebook bans for trying to raise awareness on important issues. I have been banned even for posting in related Facebook groups.

About 5 years ago I started a Facebook group called 'Question Everything' it started to get quite a large following back then, one morning, about 2 years ago I woke up and it had completely gone! Years of hard work building it up! The problem is the general masses don't know, or more to the point, don't care that this is going on!

Their freedom of speech is being eroded by the day, what these people need to realise is that if my freedom is speech is being eroded that means yours is too! My voice is YOUR voice, make the connection before its too late.

Its genius the way they have coined this term 'fake news' when, if you have read my first book 'Are You Living Or Just Existing?' you will know that the mainstream media is controlled by about 5 companies who are basically owned by western governments! Supposedly now they are 'fact checking' alternative media to class whether or not it is deemed as fake or not.

So who determines what the ultimate truth is then? That's right THEY DO! Even more laughable is that they are fact checking it against another government-owned media websites such as Snopes! So let's get this right, the truth comes from the government and to check that anything else is true or false is also decided by the government?

But of course the government is

always the pillar for truth and everyone else is just a conspiracy theorist! Surely it wouldn't be that people are finally starting to ask questions at the sheer insanity of the World and they need to cover their backsides?

Mark my words soon there won't be any way to voice an alternative opinion, that is bar walking around with a megaphone (which you would probably be tasered for in today's police state). The issue is people don't care enough for the truth, so they're generally not bothered about what is being said. They SAY they want the truth but their actions, or lack thereof, indicate that is in itself a lie.

The AI algorithms at play are quite genius, keywords are immediately flagged by their artificial intelligence so the post either gets marked down or it disappears into a cyber vacuum never to be seen again.

YouTube videos containing controversial keywords or phrases again are lost and not shown by YouTubes 'suggested videos' algorithms, as YouTube plays God and decides and pushes who and what gets seen by more people.

These social media sites are not there for your entertainment, certainly not if you're speaking out about issues, they are working out what kind of a person you are and your levels of danger to the State and its agenda. In essence, they are profiling you. Facebook is nothing more than an industrial military complex machine working out who is a threat to the deep state, and with a sea of selfies to choose from, its facial recognition AI doesn't really have much work to do as we do it for them!

The algorithms are so intelligent now that they communicate and learn from each other and thus you are profiled. The check-ins, selfies, interests etc are merely just data mining of how you look, where you are, and what kind of person you are. Don't fear though for anyone reading this who doesn't speak out against tyranny you will be safe. You're of no interest to the state, they're happy for you to drink your coffee, work a 9-5, watch sports, and get drunk at the weekend. You pose no threat to the matrix, but remember that if one person has their rights and freedom taken away then that means we all do!

Of course, it's not all just to monitor, Facebook and other platforms are obviously there to make money too so we are targeted in that way at the same time. The algorithms already have our interests, where we go, and other such data to build up the perfect consumer profile. We are then hit with adverts on our feed which relate to the profile they have built upon us. I don't know about you but I find this spooky and something I never agreed to in the first place! Its an invasion of privacy yet nobody seems to care. I was going to say next they will be invading our actual bodies but transhumanism is no joke either!

The weirdest thing happened to me not long ago and I have spoken to other people that have experienced this too. One day I was just thinking about learning to play a musical instrument, I wasn't searching for anything online I was just pondering on whether I was going to learn the guitar, drums, or harmonica? etc I wanted to fulfill this as part of my bucket list for my life. Anyways after about ten minutes I go to my phone next to me and start scrolling down my Facebook feed, to my horror there were adverts selling musical instrument learning services online!

There was no way that this could've been a coincidence, and I knew that others had experienced this, so at some level, I knew that what was actually happening was that I was the victim of some kind of mind-reading technology! Indeed if you search for this on YouTube there are people who have done experiments where they would talk about a certain subject for a day or so with their Facebook accounts open, no search anything just talk, and then they would get all these recommendations related to what they had been talking about!

So it's my theory that not only are we dealing with facial recognition, profiling, censorship, and surveillance but ultimately we are dealing with a technology humanity has not even been made aware of in thought and speech recognition. To think that your computer is reading your mind is freaky, to say the least!

The monitoring goes on as we leave the front door and our laptops, we are literally surrounded by CCTV and cameras pointing in our direction. The UK alone has more CCTV than any other Country in the World yet most people there will argue to the death that they are 'free'. Owning a car in that Country is a nightmare, if you go one mile over the speed limit you can bet your life a camera will have picked it up and you can expect a fine to come through in a couple of days, same if you park somewhere you shouldn't, with cars driving around with mobile cameras on top to catch people out. I ask myself why are these cameras and surveillance cars not pointing at the corrupt politicians in our governments who are starting illegal wars and tax evading??

All this has happened over a period of time where it has been drip fed as something normal, but it's completely wrong, why do we need to be constantly watched all the time? And don't tell me its terrorism, half of which is created and sponsored by western governments for an excuse to go and bomb more oil-rich Countries.

No, the fact is this technology is being used to enslave us further than we are already being enslaved. the average Joe on the street is targeted like he is a criminal just in case he might speak out against the real criminals that run this World. George Orwell's 1984 spoke in detail of a surveillance state, it wasn't a fairytale, he was telling us about the future.

In the coming years, I would say it will be highly likely to see drones flying about monitoring us from the skies, it will probably be sold to us as 'security' and that they are 'monitoring for terrorists' but mark my words it is to watch YOU. We are going from free-range chickens to the battery farm. No doubt it will be introduced in 'friendly' way, I've already heard the likes of

Dominoes Pizza talking about delivering food by drones, and Amazon doing the same with their goods and products.

See with anything damaging to humans there has to be a benefit to us to get us to buy into it. What better way than in this 'quick fix' convenience society to have your Hawaiian pizza delivered to your door on a Saturday night so you don't have to leave the sofa or that dress you bought for a girls night out being flown into you. Cool huh? Yes perhaps on the surface if you don't give a damn about your rights and freedoms being taken away!

Imagine sunbathing in your back garden and drones with cameras attached flying over, drones that can zoom into you and send images back to HQ. This is where its heading folks, yet I see absolutely zero resistance. People's love of technology has also clouded their judgment and everyone wants to keep ignoring the elephant in the room.

The artificial intelligence in these drones is extremely advanced, I would urge those reading this to research into 'slaughter bots' whereby using facial recognition they can home into a crowd of people and pick you out and then basically dismantle you. Drones are already used in warfare, and I very much suspect that these probably get used too in one way or another. But it goes back to what I said in the beginning, are we really to trust the people who are behind these drones? More and more people are turning against the government and the World is seeing a major shift where people just don't want or need the parasites in so-called power anymore.

Like any cornered rat there will be a time where if we don't go along willingly then it will be forced upon us.

If you're of the opinion that there is nothing wrong with this World and that things are just fine as they are then I would just stop reading now because this book won't be for you. There is an agenda playing out covertly and technology and AI is at the forefront.

AI TAKEOVER?

Ten years ago AI was something you heard about in movies, I mean we've had the technology for a while but we're now living in what I would consider a full-on science fiction movie. Don't believe me? Well just research, if you haven't already, into the robot created by Hanson Robotics called "Sophia" who it was announced a few months ago would be the first robot to be given a Saudi Arabian passport! Here we have an android so intelligent that she/he/it (who knows!) caught her creator completely off guard at a recent presentation 'joking'

that AI would 'take over the World'! The emergence of Artificial Intelligence is something people are not nearly considering enough.

Well for those of us in the know about the prominent rise of AI this was no laughing matter. See this is what these inventors don't get, they are literally playing with fire! We have reached a stage, and AI has itself, that it is now so intelligent that consciousness has now permeated it, or in layman's terms, it can now think independently for itself.

Not only is that but AI constantly learning from each other through interrelated algorithms. The soon to be released singularity.net will hugely advance this process as it acts as a cloud system where AI across the World can talk to, and learn from each other. So as AI grows so does the database and their intellectual capacity.

What annoys me about these inventors is that they don't ask the rest of the population about whether or not we want to start living amongst robots, no they just go ahead anyway! Its all about ego's and who can design the most advanced bot, no thought is being given as to what the long-term consequences of their actions are to the rest of humanity.

This would all be well and good if the long-term intentions of AI were peaceful and positive, but there is that age-old Universal law 'as above, so below' look at the level of consciousness of the creators of AI i.e HUMAN BEINGS the most selfish, destructive beings in creation right now most likely. AI is already being used for negativity, control, surveillance, and to blow people up in Wars for rich bankers! Just look at tne look at the weapons manufacturers Lockheed Martin's website, the AI they have got there to maim other human beings is terrifying! If that's not enough check out DARPA, the AI war division for the US military they have robotic drones, soldiers, and even dogs being developed to wreak havoc!

My point is that a child in its infancy takes on the habits and behavior of its parent, if it is taught from a young age to bully, control, and be violent, that's what it will become, and for me, AI has EXACTLY that same potential. And like I say it's already happening.

This rabbit hole goes way much deeper as you get into the realms of transhumanism. That's without even mentioning nanotechnology which is in most of our bodies already due to things like chemtrails, pharmaceuticals and washing up powder to name but a few. Yes, aspects of technology and AI are good, and granted I'm using it now on this laptop, but I strongly feel we really need to start considering and thinking about the other side of AI. The one which is not openly talked about and for those who benefit, for good reason.

On the subject of nanotechnology, let's go deeper into the rabbit hole, nanotechnology is essentially microscopic robots that, as I mentioned above, are already in people's body knowingly or unknowingly. This nanotechnology has the ability to think for itself, it can monitor the level of consciousness within a person, and has the ability to put the body systems out of line.

There is a huge cover-up going on about Morgellons disease with many sufferers reporting weird black technological threads and fibers underneath their skin.

Morgellons is not always a visual thing either there can also be no physical symptoms. I kind of joked earlier in the book about how the next stage is AI bodily infiltration and transhumanism, well its already going on. It's just how much you want to research into it, and how open-minded you are to having your beliefs challenged.

The evidence is overwhelming with more and more sufferers starting to come out and interestingly enough they always seem to be shut down and suppressed.

Reports are from these people is that this stuff is alive, it's conscious, and it tries to escape if you try and get rid of it. It's also self-replicating just like any other AI back up system. I appreciate this sounds far out but it is all easily researchable at the touch of a button. I guess the question is WHY? Well, transhumanism has always been about AI using humans as a host, infiltrating, and almost becoming one with the flesh of man. It seems to be highly likely that infiltration around nanotechnology seems to be the perfect way for that to happen as far out as it sounds!

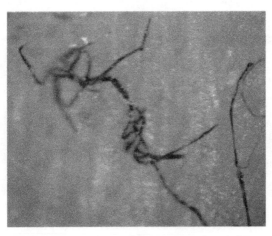

See they're always telling us what's going on too, look at films like Terminator fusing technology with man, and then you have more recently the film

Transcendence which is all about this battle with AI and how they have the ability to downloads someones consciousness onto a computer after they die, thus turning the human into an AI. I don't believe for one second that they don't already to have the technology to do this. I think this is very real, and when you consider my earlier observation on the mind reading technology, that tells me that anything is possible, and not only possible but a reality.

Transcendence

The truth is they have hidden technology from us for years, we are probably light years away from what we think we have to what we ACTUALLY do have. I'm pretty sure we have Tesla's free energy and anti-gravity, it probably doesn't even scratch the surface. We get drip fed these technologies to suit the agenda and those who call the shots. We are told we are making huge technological advancements when we have probably made them already decades ago.

So how would you feel about living in a computer? Everything you have learned, your experiences, your personality to live forever through a laptop. Sounds terrifying to me personally, no doubt they would be able to change your program too, change the output like they can on any other computer.

The ultimate betrayal for AI to use us

to create it, and then turn on us what a movie that will make, or maybe we don't even have to go to the cinema, we can see it all playing out in front of our eyes!

See there has always been a tiptoe towards transhumanism, slowly getting attached to the idea of having AI attached to us as something normal. Mobile phones we hold in our hands, then the 'hands-free' stuck to the ear, next the Google glasses stuck to the head, and now a touch screen iPhone on your arm. Does anyone question this insanity? No because they're addicted to it and they love it!

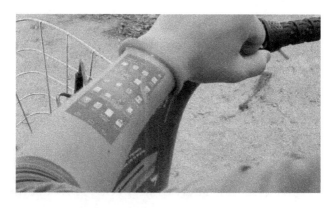

The final tiptoe towards insanity is the microchip underneath the skin, where we willingly allow AI into our bodies, that is the ultimate transhumanism goal. We've already been drip fed this to insert into our pets to help normalise it. In Sweden recently 300 commuters were microchipped to use them as railcards, why? Under the guise of 'convenience' as always, they need to sell us the benefits! what happens is that this goes out into the media and the public as to dilute the surprise from the general public when they really do want to roll them out en masse.

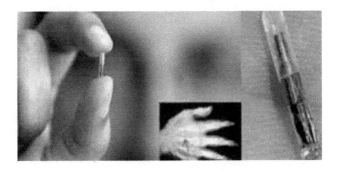

The idea of this RFID chip is all about control. Eventually, they want a one World government, with a one World monetary system, and a one World army policing it all. Everything will be on your chip how much money you have, where you spend, and what you spend it on. The implications for human freedom are massive because just say you disagree with the State, or you have a bill or tax return you haven't paid them, they can just turn the chip off. It also takes away the freedom and bartering system of cash, which is of course, a lot more difficult for them to monitor and control. I cannot help but wonder how many people who have no understanding of what REAL freedom is will rush out to get there hand chipped because they will have been sold hook, line, and sinker to all the so-called benefits.

Technology And

Health

Aside from the potential full-on transhumanism agenda playing out even if we just take technology for what it is right now we just don't really seem to question or care too much about what it is doing to our physical, emotional, and mental health. I'm talking in terms of frequencies here. We are walking around in a literal soup of WIFI and radiation, we still don't really know of the long-term damage of having mobiles with us all the time. There are reports of a rise in prostate cancer where one of the reasons cited is that men are walking around with mobiles in their pockets close to the prostate.

Human beings have a natural electromagnetic field which is being permanently messed with. It's not like you can even get away from it these days, indeed its seen as a negative if a bar or restaurant doesn't have WIFI. Overexposure to WIFI can reportedly cause insomnia and sleeping with a router or mobile phone near you can cause a lot of sleep interference.

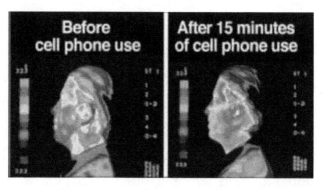

Exposure to non-thermal radio frequency radiation from Wi-Fi and cellular phones can disrupt normal cellular development, especially fetal development. A 2004 animal study linked exposure to delayed kidney development. These findings were supported by a 2009 Austrian study. In fact, the disruption of protein synthesis is so severe that authors specifically noted, "this cell property is especially pronounced in growing tissues, that is, in children and youth'

It can affect brain growth and cell function. It can impact fertility as well as neutralizing the sperm. So with all this in mind why are we begging for more, and why is it we cannot wait to get our hands on 5G where this all gets ramped up tenfold?

It has been reported that 5G has the potential to break single and double DNA strands, basically dismantling our genetic makeup. Even the World health organisation in 2011 classified radiofrequency radiation as a potential 2b carcinogen.

Although melatonin and L-Carnitine offer a nutritional defense, they don't block exposure. And that's very hard to accomplish anyway. Look at coverage maps from cell phone companies, or notice how many Wi-Fi networks your smartphone prompts for you to join. We're surrounded and bombarded by electromagnetic radiation.

Blocking exposure is difficult but there are a few small steps you can take. For one, do not keep cell phones, laptops, and tablets close to your body. And if it's not being used, shut them off (your wireless router too).

The rollout of 5G will see many smaller towers replacing the larger ones but there will be more of them and these towers will probably be about 4 feet tall, as opposed to the usual 90 feet towers currently erected around us. Cells will be available within a 100-meter range and these smart antennas will be able to differentiate between various mixed-up signals – like radio waves and WiFi signals – in the air and beam them back in an orderly fashion so to speak.

To think that we will be walking around with these mini towers all around us projecting out these frequencies is concerning, to say the least. But alas most people seem more concerned with having a secure WIFI connection than having a secure set of DNA strands! Until that changes and enough people show genuine concern you can expect this to roll out unabated.

It feels like I am the bearer of bad news, and in a way I guess I am, but surely some of us have to question this technology because based on the evidence all around us I don't think this is going to work out well. Nature doesn't make mistakes and we have our own frequencies that were designed by a much higher creative force to allow us to operate and thrive in this World. What we are seeing here is man trying to play some kind of God.

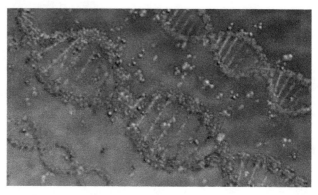

Another way that all this technology is affecting our lives in an adverse way is that we now have a permanent digital connection to the workplace. we used to have a general working day of 9-5 but now we have work laptops where many people spend their time emailing into the night. As society as a whole becomes even more connected, we can expect work to intrude ever more into our home and family lives.

Is the workaholic lifestyle stifling human creativity? I think there is now a strong argument that it is. Businesses can see when you're online, where you are, and what you're doing as 50 hour weeks are now heading up to 60 or 70 hours. This increases stress levels and can take people away from the family unit or a loving partner.

The death of human interaction is one of the most worrying aspects of our love for technology and in particular our smartphones. There seems to be a substantial rise in social anxiety amongst people these days, could it be that we have actually forgotten how to be social? Is our version of social now made up of Facebook likes or retweets?

Go to any cafe and restaurant and you will see couples or groups of people just staring down at their phones. We are connected yet disconnected at the same time. People much prefer to text now rather than pick up the phone, where genuine authentic connections can be made. Does this also tie into the fact that people don't seem to care about others anymore? Have we lost our connection and our very humanity at the same time?

While technology undoubtedly has the ability to advance us as humans, becoming over-reliant on it may actually reduce our intelligence also. For example, there are numerous examples today of drivers blindly following GPS instructions into rivers and ditches!

So what will the future give us?

Professor Stephen Hawking once said, "The development of full artificial intelligence could spell the end of the human race." Part of this risk could come from giving more military control over to Artificial Intelligence, in theory reducing the chance of human error. While it's highly unlikely full military decision making would be handed over to an AI, areas such as targeting and drone control could be put in the hands of computers.

Eventually, the human race may lose the skills it has gained over the years; with almost every aspect of our lives totally reliant on technology. The problem will come if that technology ever fails, or turns against us.

AUTOMATION

Another pressing matter nobody seems to be taking into account is how everything is now becoming automated, many industries are turning their backs on the sometimes lazy, unreliable, human workforce in place of machines and algorithms. Why wouldn't they? They don't require payment and they never take a day off sick. Let's face it that's really all corporations care about these days so why hire a human when you can hire a machine.

Just walk in your local Tescos or Asda store in the UK, where you used to see streams of checkout workers they are now being replaced with machines. Look how the travel agency industry has changed, you used to go into a physical shop to book your yearly trip, now you don't even need to leave the comfort of your own chair and you can book a flight to the Maldives within ten minutes!

Warehouse workers are now becoming under threat as large companies like Amazon invest in robots that can not only stack and shelve items, but can go and search for specific goods, collect them, and load them onto a lorry. As I mentioned earlier their goal is to drone deliver which cuts out the middleman who would deliver goods in a van.

Jobs in manufacturing are down as humans are again slowly being replaced by robots, and the technology has reached such a height that it is competitive now even with the cheapest offshore factory workers. Even a high manufacturing workforce such as China lost 15% between 1995-2002 equating to around 16 million people.

The service industry is next on the agenda with AI being developed that can flip burgers and serve customers. Sushi restaurants in Japan are now being rolled out in the west which use conveyor belts instead of waiters. There are also now touch- screen ordering systems in many fast food restaurants again obliterating the need for low paid workers who already struggle to find employment.

We are now also seeing a rise in intelligent vending machines and kiosks, again prevalent in Japan, but could this trend see the small newspaper shop on the street corner wiped out? Everything is based around profit and convenience it seems.

We are also looking at a rapid increase in the automation of cars, these cars are built with sensors that can react to different scenarios and dangers. This is combined with software that controls, navigates, and ultimately drives the vehicles. It appears top executives in the field have made it clear that most car companies are betting that automation is pretty much coming. I remember watching 'Knight Rider' in the 1980s with actor David Hasselhoff, maybe this was just another clue as to what was coming in the future! It's not even that far off the mark, we can already talk to our phones with the likes of Sirus so why not cars too? In one way this all sounds pretty cool, and let's face it some of the technology really is, but I just wonder what the spiritual connotations are from all of this.

We already have planes that are heavily automated, and mainly fly themselves bar take off and landing. You wonder whether in the future we will even have pilots in the cockpits.

Just on the spiritual side of life, quite astonishingly there is now an AI device called Muse which is a brain-sensing headband that will apparently 'elevate your meditation experience' which then provides end of session graphs and charts to map your progress! Am I missing something here? Isn't meditation supposed to be a personal spiritual experience? When did technology ever get involved with our connection to the divine? When you meditate you're opening up your mind, do we really want to allow a truckload of AI frequencies into our most precious spiritual practice? Am I the only one that finds this deeply unnatural and disturbing? What next yoga with robots? I wouldn't put it past that happening either!

Guess what folks you can soon buy a robot to have sex with too! I kid you not. If you're interested (and desperate) you can pick one up for about $20,000! They come with highly customised bodies, so don't worry if you have a certain fetish or trait that you like, you can design your sex robot with that already built in! You can even choose intellectual and personality traits such as shy, kind, and outgoing etc

The artificial intelligence in these robots has the ability to ask questions, learn, and remember, so effectively building some kind of weird artificial rapport. Even more concerning is a study showed 1 in 4 men would consider having relations with a robot within the next 50 years!

In Japan you can even have a virtual girlfriend as more and more people are giving up on dating in real life. Are we taking our love for technology to the furthest extreme? It's unreal that I'm even writing about this but its happening folks.

For any ladies reading this book don't worry there is soon to be a male version! In all seriousness, it does make me sad to think that one-day even a potential partner will be automated, how have we allowed ourselves to fall so far in our level of consciousness?

This new automated World is not just limited to robots, we now have an algorithm for pretty much everything we do online. Big data is constantly profiling us as I have already talked about. I would imagine somewhere they know everything about you just from your online activity, the question is how is this data being used?

The invasion of AI into the human job market has algorithms at the head of its arsenal. Going to the doctors could soon be a thing of the past as advanced algorithms have been developed to give you a diagnosis, and then a description once you have simply typed in your particular health issues. AI is being used to scan Xrays and diagnose, it has also been found that many times it even proves more accurate, and humans are simply being used for second opinions.

Teaching will potentially be affected as the internet becomes flooded with both online courses and algorithms that mark the student's exams and coursework. This is really appealing when you consider the thousands of pounds of debt students leave university with before they've even started their adult life.

Advanced AI could be used in court cases where there will even be no need for a jury or judge, all the evidence will be put into a machine, and then the machine will decide if you go to prison and how long for!

It makes you wonder what we are all going to do for work in the coming years, we have already seen a massive reduction in jobs across the board, when you take into account the rise of the robots, you can really only see this continuing in that vein.

Of course, the plus side is that much of this can make our lives easier and more convenient but at what cost? Aliens are not outside of this Planet, they're already here and they've infiltrated under the radar as we have become lost in the love affair with the alien itself.

TONY SAYERS

CONCLUSION AND

SOLUTIONS

The whole point of this book was to really bring to light the whole picture of technology and artificial intelligence. All we are ever told is how good it is, how we are at the forefront of something amazing and you only need to scratch the surface to understand this is far from the case.

I have spent years researching this topic and people are just ignoring the elephant in the room as I said earlier. Everything I have spoken about is very real and going on right under our noses. Our judgments have been massively clouded as technology has flirted with us.

We see its very best side and we have fallen into a love amnesia with it, but what about our humanity, our spirituality, our hearts, and our need to interact and connect with each other on a physical and emotional level?

We are connected but yet so disconnected at the same time. It concerns me greatly that we already live in a World where people care little for the environment, nature, the oceans, and the rainforests. Just how disconnected from what's actually real will the next generation be? This 'selfie generation'?

I also worry about the next generations walking around and having their brains and DNA scrambled by WIFI towers everywhere.

It really goes back to my original point of the level of consciousness this technology is being created from. Humans are not a peaceful population, we have not transcended from wars and weapons yet.

We have not stopped serving merely the ego, and if the creators are at this level of consciousness this AI is clearly so intelligent that it will learn to be how we are which is concerning

If I felt that we were at a good point in human evolution for all these robots then I would be writing a very different book. We have already seen with the nanotechnology that there is already a malevolence about it, and if this stuff can learn and start to think independently of itself then who knows where that could end up.

My aim has been to simply get people to think, look at both sides of the coin here, look at the angles that we are not told about, look at your children and your grandchildren, how do you see a technology run World shaping their personalities and futures?

This is the problem we are not thinking, we are either too busy, or we want to remain in ignorance. The World is the home for all of us so we have both an individual and collective responsibility to take care of it.

A big part of the solution is how we bring up the next generations, we need to maintain their connection with what is real and nature itself. We have to encourage real-life connection. We have to lead by example in this sense. I know technology is here to stay and it will expand, but lets at least keep some of the parts that make us human.

We need to talk about this issue, just talking about it raises awareness, it gets other people thinking which people are just not doing in enough numbers. Once we get people thinking about this we can then make choices.

Just saying no and rejecting certain aspects of this issue can help, choosing stores that are not automating their business, for example, making small conscious choices. Turning the mobile phones off at the dinner table, the little changes in your daily life that maintain who we really are.

A big part of the solution is how we bring up the next generations, we need to maintain their connection with what is real and nature itself. We have to encourage real-life connection. We have to lead by example in this sense. I know technology is here to stay and it will expand, but lets at least keep some of the parts that make us human.

We need to talk about this issue, just talking about it raises awareness, it gets other people thinking which people are just not doing in enough numbers. Once we get people thinking about this we can then make choices.

Just saying no and rejecting certain aspects of this issue can help, choosing stores that are not automating their business, for example, making small conscious choices. Turning the mobile phones off at the dinner table, the little changes in your daily life that maintain who we really are.

Turn your WIFI router off at night and any mobile phones. There are also other ways of protecting against EMFs such as orgonite and certain crystals like selenite and black tourmaline

Research into where your nearest mobile phone towers are so you don't put yourself right in harm's way. And help join the resistance against 5G.

Most of all take action and get active in your community with awareness we have the ability to shield ourselves from some of this, and collectively we can all make a difference.

If you enjoyed this book please consider giving me a review on Amazon, it really does help with my work and to get the message out there to other people.

You can also join my weekly mailing list where I talk about other issues that affect our World, it will also put you ahead of the game when it comes to new talks, podcasts, and book launches you can subscribe here

https://transcendingtimes.org/subscribe-to-newsletters/

Feel free to check out my other books here 'Are You Living Or Just Existing?' 'Ten Life Hacks To Beat The Matrix' and 'NOFAP'. All are available as Kindle or paperback on Amazon.

https://transcendingtimes.org/books/